ANN MORRIS

BREAD · BREAD · BREAD

PHOTOGRAPHS BY
KEN HEYMAN

SCHOLASTIC INC.

NEW YORK TORONTO LONDON AUCKLAND SYDNEY

ISBN 0-590-44342-9

Text copyright © 1989 by Ann Morris.
Photographs copyright © 1989 by Ken Heyman.
All rights reserved. Published by Scholastic Inc.,
730 Broadway, New York, NY 10003, by arrangement with
Lothrop, Lee & Shepard Books, a division of William
Morrow & Company.

12 11 10 9 8 7 6 5 4 3 2 1   1 2 3 4 5 6/9

Printed in the U.S.A.   08

First Scholastic printing, January 1991

BREAD · BREAD · BREAD

5

People eat
bread all over
the world.

There are many kinds, many shapes, many sizes—

skinny bread,

fat bread,

round flat bread,

bread with a hole,

9

crunchy bread,
lunchy bread…

10

and bread
to soak up
your egg.

Pizza, pretzel...they are bread too.

Bread on the table…

bread on your head.

Bread is good for you.

It helps
you grow.

It makes
you strong.

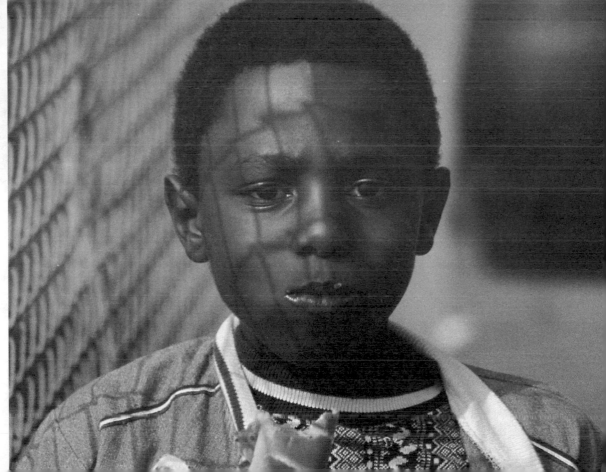

Making bread, shaping bread,

baking bread,

toasting bread,

cooking bread over the fire.

Fill up
the basket…

off to the market.

Bread for sale!

Breaking bread together...

Have a bite…
delicious!

INDEX

Title page ISRAEL: Fat loaves for sale are stacked by the wall of the Old City of Jerusalem.

5 UNITED STATES: Sliced bread topped with peanut butter and jelly is a favorite with American children.

6 PERU: A little boy munches a piece of the typical Peruvian bread that his mother sells at the local market.

7 GHANA: A tasty roll curbs an African boy's appetite until dinnertime.

7 ENGLAND: Another tasty roll does the same for a little girl thousands of miles from Africa.

8 INDONESIA: This American-style sliced white bread is made by a bakery in Surabaya, Indonesia.

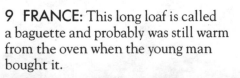

9 FRANCE: This long loaf is called a baguette and probably was still warm from the oven when the young man bought it.

9 FRANCE: These small French loaves are for making sandwiches.

9 ISRAEL: Pita is a bread with a pocket that can hold almost all of a meal.

9 PORTUGAL: This doughnut-shaped loaf is sprinkled with sesame seeds before baking.

10 UNITED STATES: Pizza, inspired by Italian breads baked with sauces on them, has become almost as American as apple pie.

10 FRANCE: These three friends enjoying a Sunday afternoon picnic are firm believers that a good sandwich starts with crusty, freshly baked French bread.

11 INDIA: This Sikh family in Bombay use chappatties, a kind of unleavened wheat bread, to soak up their egg. In Indian tradition, it is good manners to eat with your fingers.

12 UNITED STATES: Another pizza eaten on the run. Pizza can be topped with tomatoes, cheese, sausages, peppers—any or all of these—plus a variety of other toppings.

13 GERMANY: A pretzel is made from a stiff dough of flour, water, and salt, and twisted into this characteristic shape.

14 PORTUGAL: Hard rolls are an essential part of a splendid meal in an outdoor cafe.

15 SICILY: This girl is carrying bread baked in an old-fashioned oven to the village main square, where it will be sold.

16 GREECE: This bread maker obviously enjoys the taste of her own bread, made from hand-milled flour and baked in an outdoor village oven.

17 UNITED STATES: Rolls especially made to hold hot dogs help make a meal for this Los Angeles boy on his way to a baseball game.

18 UNITED STATES: Making bread includes measuring, kneading, rising, punching, shaping, and baking.

20 UNITED STATES: A modern toaster for sliced bread does the job quickly and evenly.

20 ITALY: Bread toasted outdoors at a Gypsy camp smells and tastes wonderful.

21 MEXICO: Tortillas are a thin, flat bread that is baked on an open griddle.

22 ECUADOR: The woman is carrying the bread she made that morning to the market, where she will sell it to the people in the village.

22 PERU: This bread, just dumped from its baking tray into a basket, may look messy, but it tastes very good.

23 ISRAEL: This man uses a bicycle cart to bring his bread to market.

24 ISRAEL: This large raised loaf made of whole grains with a hole in the middle is popular in the Middle East.

25 HONG KONG: Several of the breads in this Hong Kong shop have sweet fillings in them.

25 GUATEMALA: Though the mother baked the bread, everyone in the family gets involved in arranging the loaves for sale.

26 ISRAEL: A Tel Aviv family celebrate the Sabbath by breaking bread together. Prayers are said over the special bread, called challah, at the beginning of the Sabbath meal.

29 UNITED STATES: There's nothing like home-baked bread!

◆◆◆◆◆◆◆◆◆◆◆◆◆◆◆◆◆◆◆◆ ANN MORRIS ◆◆◆◆◆◆◆◆◆◆◆◆◆◆◆◆◆◆◆◆◆

has taught young children in both private and public New York City schools, and has also taught at Teachers College, Columbia University; New York University; and Bank Street College of Education. She left the teaching field to become editorial director of the Early Childhood Department of Scholastic, Inc., where she produced a number of award-winning films, film-strips, and other audiovisual materials. She now devotes full time to writing and developing children's books. Among her recent titles are *Night Counting, Sleepy Sleepy,* and *Cuddle Up.*

◆◆◆◆◆◆◆◆◆◆◆◆◆◆◆◆◆◆◆◆ KEN HEYMAN ◆◆◆◆◆◆◆◆◆◆◆◆◆◆◆◆◆◆◆◆◆

is widely recognized as a foremost photojournalist. A student of Margaret Mead, he coauthored two books with her, *Family* and *World Enough.* His photographs have appeared in many other books, including *The Family of Children,* a book about childhood around the world, and *The World's Family.* His photographs in these books have earned him the reputation as one of the world's most sensitive interpreters of the human condition.